Roswell

Judith Roitman

Roswell

Judith Roitman

Judith Roitman's suite of documentary-poetic lyrics, *Roswell*, parses elements of narrative fact/fallacy. Take-off point is New Mexico, 1947, intersection of flying saucer crash reports and coverups. Redacted, randomized, resurrected texts jigsaw a story that is or could be. The poet is storyteller for a script that continuously shapeshifts. Words are reassigned in each moment of this essential collection.

Denise Low, winner Red Mountain Editor's Choice Award

What are we looking at? That is the question that Judith Roitman's fascinating *Roswell* poses to "eyewitnesses" and readers alike. Whether through a narrative debris field of testimonies, articles, and reports, or from the point of view of an abject alien in the desert, that elusive "it" is "seen as wished for never more than never recognized." Ultimately, Roitman's compelling poems are about that which seems alien, other, only partially experienced, when the "positive malfunctioned." In other words, this is a book about 2018 as much as 1947. You need to read it.

Joseph Harrington, author of *Of Some Sky*

Judith Roitman's *Roswell* makes me wonder whether it's possible for humans to engage aliens without the former humanizing the latter. The poems, after all, claim "surviving alien remembers its descendants," "surviving alien remembers nourishment," and so on as if the human Roitman can inhabit non-earthling point of views. Such may be considered empathy. But for these poems relating to 1947 events to come out in 2018 is also to emphasize how little empathy is displayed today by the U.S. administration for "aliens" of a different sort but within the same species. How far humanity has fallen. These poems accomplish what good poems do: go beyond themselves into other matters as they make the reader think.

Eileen R. Tabios, author of *Love In A Time of Belligerence*

ISBN-13: 978-0-9883891-5-1

Acknowledgments: Some of these poems have appeared in *Otoliths*, *Eleven Eleven*, and *E.ratio.*

Cover Design: Wendy Glaess

theenk Books
107 Washington Street
Palmyra, New York 14522

To order: http://theenkBooks.com

Contact: theenkbooks@twc.com

Also distributed by Small Press Distribution
1341 Seventh StreetBerkeley, CA 94710
http://www.spdbooks.org

to Stan

Table of contents:

Humans	1 - 34
Aliens	35 - 62
Afterword and Sources	64 - 66

Humans

[sighting by Kenneth Arnold, June 24, 1947, between Mineral and Yakima, Washington]

bright left north Mt. Rainier fast speed [not] window reflections [not] reflections [not] long chain geese [not]new jet [no] tail

dark profile bright light flashes flipped thin flat almost invisible series convex shapes crescent saucers initial saucer disc pie pan half moon convex thin behind disappeared

gauge compare angular size details distance similar 10 days absolute size larger greater 100 feet estimate 140 to 280 feet human visual acuity

grouped diagonally stepped-down echelon five miles level horizontal weaved darting around peaks occasionally flip bank unison blindingly bright flashes

parallel open window objects unobstructed not disappear rapid continuous forward 50 miles one minute forty-two seconds over 1700 miles per hour three times any conservative round down 1200

regardless [of] origin
destination
whoever controlled
impossible survive
controlled elsewhere
no doubt
unknown to earth

[teletype sent by FBI Dallas to SAC Cincinnati]

FLYING DISC INFORMATION **BLACKEDOUT BLACKEDOUT BLACKEDOUT** TELEPHONICALLY ADVISED THIS OFFICE PURPORTING RECOVERED THIS DATE THIS DISC HEXAGONAL SUSPENDED BY CABLE WHICH BALLOON APPROXIMATELY TWENTY FEET DIAMETER **BLACKEDOUT BLACKEDOUT BLACKEDOUT** FURTHER ADVISED OBJECT FOUND RESEMBLES BUT TELEPHONIC CONVERSATION BETWEEN NOT BORNE OUT TRANSPORTED FOR EXAMINATION INFORMATION PROVIDED NATIONAL INTEREST ATTEMPTING BREAK STORY ADVISE **BLACKEDOUT BLACKEDOUT BLACKEDOUT** WOULD REQUEST WRIGHT FIELD ADVISE NO FURTHER INVESTIGATION

WYLY RECORDED

END

ACK IN ORDER

DPI HS

[Lydia A .Sleppy interview]

I had been cut off [they were] gonna load it up take to Texas John had been out there I got into it enough pretty big story took [the rest] in shorthand "FBI you will cease transmitting" anything newsworthy put on [teletype] machine Lambertz watch[ed] bell [signaling interruption] call from John McBoyle had seen them take thing away planes from Wright Field something hot

[Roswell Daily Record July 8 1947]

in sight less than a minute
disappeared over treetops
northwesterly direction
two inverted saucers
washbowls placed together
glowing object
heard no sound
ran into yard
40 to 50 seconds
glowed from inside
not merely underneath
capture[d] flying saucer
announced at noon
high rate of speed
swishing sound
recovered disk
called attention
came into view

[what W.W. (Mac) Brazel saw on the J.B. Foster ranch, from the Roswell Daily Record July 9]

large as a table top
did not know size or shape
no strings or wire
tape with flowers
rubber strips, tinfoil, tough paper, sticks
rubber smoky gray scattered
letters on some parts
no words found
scotch tape
one paper fin
eyelet [:] attachment [?]
maybe five pounds
tinfoil paper tape sticks bundle about three feet long
rubber bundle 18 or 20 inches long
large area of bright wreckage
did not see fall from sky
did not see before torn up
no sign of metal
no sign of propellers
not weather balloon
could not reconstruct
[could not] make kite
could not put back [together]

[Bessie Brazel Schreiber & William Brazel Jr., children of Mac Brazel, testify on what their father brought home]

like aluminum foil tape stuck to some pieces could not be peeled or removed something on the order of tinfoil wouldn't tear wrinkle it, lay it back down, resumed shape pliable couldn't crease or bend it [permanently] like a plastic but metallic also what appeared like heavily waxed paper also [something] like a pipe sleeve four inches across and long with flange also threadlike material like silk not silk very strong no strands or fibers more like wire all one piece or substance on the order of heavy gauge monofilament fishing line I couldn't break it also wooden-like like balsa wood in weight but darker and harder pliable but wouldn't break weighed nothing you couldn't scratch it no writing or markings some pieces like numbers/lettering no words to make out written out like numbers columns didn't not numbers we use

Dad said Army said not anything made by us Dad said figures on some pieces like petroglyphs

I picked this stuff up might be two or three days or a week took it out put it in a cigar box happened to notice put that piece of foil in that box the damn thing just started unfolding just flattened out weird couldn't tear it color between tinfoil and lead foil about the thickness I got to playing with it I'd fold it crease it lay it down [it would] unfold couldn't tear it

everybody was asking — oh, I picked up — I dunno I rode out there I was riding through I was looking that's why I found not over a dozen maybe eight but only three different

lo and behold here comes the military "I've got a cigar box" "we came after those" "you can have it no use for it at all."

[Walt Whitmore Jr., Jesse Marcel, Jesse Marcel Jr. on debris]

small beams extremely light in weight purple I-beams number added [?] no dent symbols [could not be] cut definite[ly] cannot writing vast area covered exploded more geometric-type could not interpret nondescript debris how it stands don't know what it was metal thin weight practically nothing tried sledge hammer could not be burned like parchment won't bend hieroglyphic symbols [columns] 16 pound sledge hammer scattered something meant we didn't know woodlike can't dent tried [to] bend pink and purple tried [to] dent tried [to] burn embossed inner surfaces like lead foil [could not be] torn tried [to] bend would not burn like tinfoil appearance could not be broken wouldn't bend just picked up fragments configuration multiplied[?] lavender

[Sheridan W Cavitt testifies about debris and disposition of it]

accompany[ied] Rickett and Marcel
[to] ranchland area [to] recover material
area very small no gouge or crater
resemble[d] bamboo type square sticks very light
metallic reflecting material very light
material consistent with weather balloon
easily fit into one vehicle
taken to Eighth Air Force Fort Worth
subsequently identified as weather balloon
did not make report since not a big deal
did not merit written report
reputed never there never happened
seems to imply conspiratorial more likely wasted time
only went once recovered debris once
no[thing] secretive or security or unusual
do not recall incident mentioned again
never thought of it until contacted
do not recall hitting with sledgehammers
did not test for radioactivity
do not recall burn[ing] but wife
recall[s] Marcel wife and son held over fire when cookout
not part of conspiracy
never sworn to secrecy
no classified information withholding
never threatened by US Government not to talk
whole incident no big deal did not involve extraterrestrial

[Robert Porter on transporting material]

one triangle rest smaller shoebox-size
brown paper tape fit car trunk
Fort Worth Wright Field maintenance lunch B-25

[Robert E. Smith 1991 interview]

hanger unusual flatbeds [filled] entire plane inspectors lot of people wasn't heavy crate[s] plainclothes strangers MP's on outskirts truck convoy crashed planes not flown out east side of ramp unusual strange object officially crashed plane largest [crate] 20 feet long 4 to 5 feet high 4 to 5 feet side rest 2 or 3 feet long 2 feet square or smaller dollies planes involvement help[ed] load crates of debris headed north loading 6 perhaps 8 hours personnel different from military ID indication something serious not plane crash farm dirt hangar on east end aware event when hangar armed guards load crates UFO mechanical problems sirens headed over red lights checked width height something else

[Irving Newton is called into General Ramey's office to identify wreckage]

balloon RAWIN target
many launched
ground radar
altitude familiar
rubber expandable
launched altitude
target approximately
ball and jacks metallic
balsa wood kite sticks
weather faded

interviewed
quoted
misquoted
facts remain

[Bill Rickett reporting on tour of crash site with Lincoln LaPaz]

animals affected animals strange

touched down taken off
sand glass-like metal thin foil stuff

people seen two fly slowly low altitude
day or two after other

trouble touched down repairs
taken off exploded
more than one

positive malfunctioned
leave speculations out

[Walter Haut affidavit]

only heads extended beyond not quite wide contour 10 year old child heads larger not [see] features personally observed from distance bodies

second site messages stacked no identif[ication] permitted observe heavy guard temporary morgue handled egg shape no windows [etc.] debris field 6 feet high 12 to 15 length surface metallic

attention diverted two separate teams flying disc too many civilians office inundated deliver news release downed vehicle wreckage unlike any civilian report convinced from outer space

[F.B., Army Air Forces photographer]

they [were] picking up pieces
they'd open it up you'd take a picture
take picture fifteen feet away
went to the next spot
almost blind because sunny
couldn't hardly see
telling us what to do
take a picture of this
moved in a circle taking pictures
thin
lying on a tarp
bodies under a canvas
dark complected
awful dark
couldn't hardly see
too big of a head
[bodies] just about identical
four bodies I could see
smelled funny
closed tent
about twenty by thirty foot

[Gerald Anderson sees a craft and creatures in the Plains of San Augustin while on a rock-hunting trip with his father, brother, and uncle, when he is 5 years old]

goddam spaceship large shiny silver object embedded two creatures laying obviously dead something moving movement underneath [brother and uncle] trying to communicate two not moving movement down there sheets laid out one creature writhing [one] creature sitting cross-legged see moving underneath [creature] look[ed] from one to the next hand up [in] front of face [at] first [creature was] afraid look[ed] from one to the next

ones [lying] on ground eyes closed one-piece uniform obviously uniforms skin like grey glove leather color of porpoise stuff hanging out whipping coming out of gash disc incredibly cold foil couldn't cut with knife wouldn't burn material in box container closer to disc colder [I was] standing next to dead another next to it I reached out and touched I didn't touch skin

chemical smell unfold ridgeline west side arroyo underneath chilly

turned and looked straight at me BAM impact out of control fall huge eyes right at me trying to tell me something another crash BAM felt impact another impact rumbling sound sudden stop

I ran [they] weren't people climbed ridgeline west side arroyo huge elliptical gash [Army] vehicles moving skids marks windmill

[Lieutenant governor Joe Montoya as told by Ruben Anaya]

saucer
mouth [like] knife-cut across
not human
[n]ever tell
large bald heads
not from this world
big eyes shaped
one alive could hear
larger than
one alive
don't know
so skinny
four little
don't know
not helicopter
not believe
four thin fingers
short
large heads
not human
skinny

[mortician Glenn Dennis is queried on preserving bodies found in the desert]

two mangled
one good shape
some time ago
laid out in July
what's this going to do
in prairie
blood system
tissue
going to be dark
going to be bad
exposed to elements
how to move
[suggested] dry ice
[no] indication where they were
didn't want ambulance
[not] in vehicle
separated by two or three miles
[no] indication

[Glenn Dennis testifies what unnamed nurse saw during autopsy]

cartilage [not] teeth   lower portion crushed
horrible   skulls flexible   eyes deeply set   no
fingernails   mouth slit   gruesome   skin black
ears flaps   head large   smell   nose concave
no hair   suction cups [at] end of fingers

skin black   mouth slit   smell gruesome   ears
flaps   horrible   eyes deeply set   skulls flexible
cartilage [not] teeth   suction cups [at] end of
fingers   head large   nose concave   no hair
no fingernails   lower portion crushed

no hair   horrible   gruesome   suction cups [at]
end of fingers   skulls flexible   nose concave
smell   lower portion crushed   no fingernails
skin black   head large   ears flaps   cartilage
[not] teeth   eyes deeply set   mouth slit

smell gruesome   no hair   mouth slit   no
fingernails   nose concave   lower portion
crushed   skin black   head large   cartilage [not]
teeth   horrible   suction cups [at] end of fingers
ears flaps   skulls flexible   eyes deeply set

[Gerald Anderson on the military appearing]

standing how without us hearing they knew rounded get away shouting last thing say get in everywhere sudden[ly] hear they run us off staff car flatbed truck ambulances arguing soldiers scary last thing truck looking back aircraft they knew walk up soldier never heard guns invasion force no doubt shoot machine gun drive crane out of nowhere didn't react guy exactly like soldiers military never heard dirt highway pointing marked getaway

[Barbara Dugger speaks of her grandfather George the sheriff and her grandmother Inez who ran for sheriff]

someone came told him went to site
four space beings heads large one alive suits silk
thought best [for] country not to talk
grandmother ran lost [said] don't tell
be killed entire family killed

[Loretta Proctor and Marian Strickland talk about whether Mac Brazel was bribed and/or threatened]

insulted mis-used disrespected Mac wouldn't talk
a man who had integrity wouldn't report it
kicked around moved to Alamogordo or Tularosa
put in a locker a large refrigerated building you had a
key

[my] husband saw Mac surrounded by Air Force
[said] if he ever saw something else
threatened if opened mouth back side of jail definitely
they walked right by and Mac wouldn't speak

you could get your beef out
how could he with rancher's wages
worse than annoyed
after he come back home not supposed to tell

[Richard M. Neal, Jr., M.D. FOIA request]

medical directory pathological examinations authentic photocopies full body close-up flesh higher mineral content denser bones pathological (post-mortem) (comparative) greater interest recover 4 aliens size 10 year old boy examined laboratory bodies as small humanoid tan (or sunburned) disclosed human skeleton two extra ribs each side rumors post-mortem performed on alien bodies

release information for secure study crashed authentic 9 page (1947) exempt mandatory under FOIA because this past separate portion found from rest debris great interest extra-terrestrial object would/does not interfere knowledge would give specifically effects suffered secondary

positive success primitive communications with established mission establish communications with met two at pre-arranged location in after discovery prompted President appoint managed exchange basic probably last (firsthand) experienced pathologist radiologist neurophysiologist cardiovascular-thoracic aliens restricted limited number such as lasted approximately three presently living one of participated Guggenheim Foundation 23rd Street New York City Project Whirlwind MIT 1947 then referred many lectures seminars scheduled herald committee twelve individuals “Majestic-12”

could subliminal suggestions or possibly to prepare why decided this 45th year eventually to regards movies to cushion believed continuing over 75% believes this serious believe wishes know truth of leaking some optimistic while anticipate nevertheless value enclosed brief synopsis please review respectfully requesting realize reluctant giving approach positive will respect confidentiality anonymity hopeful sympathetic to

[combined history of 509th Bomb Group and Roswell Army Air Field,
1 July 1947 through 31 July 1947]

pursuant to command this date
significant changes activation de-activation this chapter
Jennings assumed Blanchard on leave
Horton assigned Bowman transferred replaced by Jones
Arner assumed relieved Bohanan
new Lucas assumed relieved Kingsbury assumed
formerly Lucas
Hilburn transferred replaces Casey on orders
briefings simulating briefing large group representing
historical section seriously handicapped removal
stenographer
quality reports inadequate lectures prepared properly
train liaisons
quite busy month answering flying disc reported
turned out radar tracking balloon
main project successful air force day
arrangements Blanchard visit Governor declare
host senior air scouts several visiting
several easy chairs and couches more comfortable
public information commanding guests Kiwanis
talk future very well received
arrangements call public information crash calls
in accordance regulations too late any good
3rd photo laboratory transferred principal difficulty
lack of photostat paper
following breakdown work
visitors

[Marcia J. van Note 1994 memorandum on record management procedures]

DoD Directive designates central liaison for enclosed describes specific tasking and primary received enclosed official on subject effort GAO work review request requested management procedures crash incident facts regarding reported appeared episode requests attributed

anxious respond dispel unresponsive important identify correct enclosed not mention incident site interest unable determine appropriate scheduled meeting entrance meeting clarify issues primary action office identified provide if not available reached

[Robert J. McCormick 1994 memorandum request for records and directives]

Department Defense other review whether handling retention disposition investigation reporting incidents similar fulfill Air Force portion requested identify directives records retention disposition reporting investigations wreckage/ debris retention disposition records air vehicle impacts crashes identify records groups indexes associated provide copies provide (interim or final)

[James L. Cole memorandum: GAO records management procedures of crash incidents]

same subject identified directives concerning crashes response one within purview other managed

guidance investigations not release mishap prevention only air vehicle mishap not cover crashes other branches

guidance investigation normally releasable claims litigation boards convened disciplinary obtain evidence administrative preserve evidence

anticipated litigation wreckage/debris retention normally safety investigation retain advantageous wreckage disposition paragraph 10 publicity not require[d] responsibility manages retention others disposed

searched microfilm mishaps period only are

A-26C 7 miles nw Hobbs
P-51N 7 miles nw Hobbs
C-82A 7 miles se Albuquerque
NM P-80A Carrizozo
NM PQ-14B 15 miles sw Alamagordo

extended rule 4 directs destroy air mishaps other government civilian note involving unmanned reports not retained no information

[Air force report: files and records searched]

LeMay Papers
Spaatz Papers
Twining Papers
Vandenberg Papers
Air Adjutant General
Records of Army Air
IG Report — Individuals
IG Correspondence
02 Intel Records
Records of the Army
HQ USAF Messages
Top Secret MSGS
Office of Director
HQ USAF Records
A.P. Crary Papers

[Air Force report: locations searched for files and records]

White Sands — Army
Air Defense School Ft. Bliss
Bolling AFB
Pentagon
Watson Labs
8th AF
SAC
10th AF Brooks AFB
Bolling AFB
426 AAFBU Kirtland AFB
Kirtland AFB
Bolling FLD Command
Bolling FLD
3151 Elec Grp Watson Labs
Wright Pat
Joint Long Range Prov Grd
Air Weather Serv ADW
HQ AMC Wright Pat
10th AF
Cambridge Labs
3069 Exp Tex GO Holloman AFB
CONAF Mitchel FLD
12th AF
409th Bomb Group
427 AAFBU

[Project Mogul and sound channels in ocean and atmosphere]

upward angles frequency increases sound channel radio transmitters detect halfway around world about 45,000 feet signals researched oceans propagate microphones similar axis accepted explanation speed sourced waves downward region toward minimum moderately successful sound waves

theorized increases typical large extraordinary ranges wave nearly on axis speed minimum detected stay refraction upper atmosphere refracted back sound focused absorption increases lower sound speed receiver placed audibility from 0 to 25 from 90 to 25 balloons superseded

long-distance detection less 12° waves refracted angles sound waves Soviet bomb tests relay long ranges refracted back waves less 12° final pulse loudest signals characteristic exceed accepted ranges thus sound channel decreases to axis height zone of silence 25 to 90 both located triangulation

[Athelstan Spilhaus, Charles Moore, and Albert Trakowski describe the construction and deployment of Project Mogul balloons]

General Mills polyethelene neoprene degradation dark gray black ashes early neoprene Kaysam mold Dewey dip type Winzen St. Paul Minnesota Dewey Almy Cambridge toy manufacturer translucent translucent milky to dark extruded difficult to tear polyethelene (non-stretchable) Kaysam some toy/novelty company

arcs flower circles diamonds pinkish radar reflectors corner reflectors sheets of reflective more fragile twisted nylon lines radar reflectors radiosondes covered with white painted cardboard 307(C) aluminized paper debris symbols fabric sticky paper braided no monofilament tape reinforcements gouges (shallow) various strings wooden beams balsa wood dragging metalized paper reflectors of tracking whatever we had eyelets sonobouys cover with metal reinforcing tape 307(B) aluminum foil Elmers-like glue

multiple radar targets not cordon anti-oxidants microphone not coordinate no great effort expendable flight #4 launched balloons documentation July 8th press releases July 10th Alamagordo News reflectors scattered depending on acrid plasticizers no planned cover story no contact with multiple balloons and targets sonobouy (black box?) not recall no documentation

[Summary of HQ NAIC Research]

FINDINGS

conversations did not turn up
AFIT Library Base Library
Wright State University holdings
Dayton, Centerville, Woodbourne Public Libraries
congressional investigations
review all UFO-related material
transferred National Archives
encompassing several million pages
made available to public
did not turn up reference Roswell
[did not turn up] presence of flying saucer(s) and/or alien(s)
electronic search
did not turn up conclusive evidence

CONCLUSIONS

based on absence of documentation
always those who say "you didn't search"
always those who say "we know you are not revealing"
several hundred man-years of effort
every reasonable avenue of research exhausted
convinced no such record
Roswell material if it [existed] was nothing remarkable
standard procedure retired or destroyed
if extraterrestrial would [be] preserved
believe nothing extraterrestrial found
concerted research failed to turn up evidence

despite best efforts not one scrap
earliest UFO books do not mention
Condon report [does] not mention
Blue Book records do not mention
[not] one incontestable photograph
so long ago no record trail
can never be definitely resolved

Aliens

[scenario in which children encounter a wounded alien in the desert and are cruel]

mouth in hand small mouth cavity goes nowhere no tubes no vocal no digestive no breathing none — hand in mouth many hands in mouth small child hands pulling what does it do does it do mouth no teeth no saying no tongue just mouth cavity no lips why bother why appear many hands poking small child hands eyes cannot flap no lids big eyes all pupils how do you know where it is looking you would feed it something but how would it eat?

[scenario in which the surviving alien is seen at the edge of a trailer park]

in peripheral vision first thought
someone's child could not believe
disappeared behind then appeared
one skinny limb then another
maybe arm maybe leg naked
twilight couldn't tell color
big head dog didn't move
didn't bark so still dog
almost shaking if I blink
gone but wasn't

[scenario in which aliens live in underground complexes built by the U.S Army]

find within each other
swarm did not know so many
such smooth
tunnels machines
reconstructed
Other present watching
Other control secret
pact mutuality not
mutual do not
stumble across this

[scenario in which the surviving alien advises the president and cabinet in the White House]

in suit
in tie
in corners
fluttering
half-seen
center
at edges
with gaze
behind curtain
behind door
fugitive
unexplained
ubiquitous
unexplained
phantom
unexplained
unnoticed
unexplained

[scenario in which aliens appear in tv sitcom as themselves]

eyes difficult special lenses protect
also suckers problematic sticking furniture
uniforms easily reproduced
voice-over needed sync to
audience spontaneously
as stumble lurch such large head

[scenario in which aliens move among us undetected]

projecting image into mind fluid unrelenting what seen expected deviation unnoticed as in mall so even jostled unnoticed such small feet unnoticed what reached for what currency on elevator reaching seen as wished for never more than never recognized seen as what expected exactly what

[the surviving alien in the moments just before and of the crash]

context shift unimagined
uncontrollable controls shift
controls useless any thought
of holding together gone
all parts severed each its own
each meeting its own
contact severed no orientation
strange gravity strange light

[the surviving alien surveys dead and dying comrades]

suction diagnostic no cure
no tools no signal
one part holds another
parts vanishing perhaps weak
parts vanishing only this part left

[the surviving alien attempts to breathe]

through skin
between mesh
skin-plates
strange atmosphere
unnourishing
skin spaces expand
take more in
more what not what
needed can't not
do it as if
searching as if
opening would help
search

[the surviving alien remembers nourishment]

how it would sit in the mouth absorbed through membranes
held against digestive membrane the slow pleasure of it
seeping across digestive membrane

one substance used again and again
so many to nourish such satisfaction seeping inward
shared such multiple all aspects

[the surviving alien tries to make sense of things]

can't say colors atmosphere ground

can't say barrier nourish where where-are when

can't escape body
can't escape

[the surviving alien surveys its surroundings]

light wrong
gravity wrong
color wrong
ground wrong
atmosphere wrong

can't say: wrong
can't say: things
can't say: what
can't say: where
can't say: where are

dry things everything dry
creature not creature
can't say: creature
can't say: not creature
no way knowing

other parts not moving
other parts voiceless
other parts gone
one part slight motion
tending to it
tending useless
outstretched appendage
appendage useless

[the surviving alien observes humans talking]

bottom of faces
moving without
ingestion pressure
waves what
formulation what
function

[the surviving alien's clothing is removed]

without what can what protect
supplementary gases gone without
filter gone all raw no protect
no supplement disintegration
cut through no protect disintegrate
line cut peeled substance touching
causing disintegration line cut
line appearing disintegration
not with taken what can

[the surviving alien remembers its descendants]

within suction between sudden existence coming into own laid down in barrels laid up nutrients bathing enclosures first small then larger watching being watched watching being watched

[the surviving alien tries to communicate with its peers]

no whom to communicate

can’t get out make sense escape

not received nothing received sent not received
as if walls

can’t be found

can’t get out
inside body
ricochet
inside body
bounce

if sent who would believe
full stop

if sent who would receive
full stop

[the surviving alien communicates with its human companion]

Other not penetrate
incomplete offering
only small pieces
never absent
half formation
missing
always never shifting
from here reach deflected
so much not
without from here
transparent
Other so much missing
not comprehended

[the surviving alien places its hands in the streams of Rendija Canyon and Pueblo Canyon, Los Alamos]

immersed
planetary message flow
what telling
as if could
as molecules slip
one then another
distinct, each distinct
coherent
linked
telling

[the surviving alien walks under pine trees in dry desert air]

each needle
: terpene :
pinene 20 carbon
16 hydrogen
: ester :
bornyl acetate 12 carbon
20 hydrogen
2 oxygen
infused gas
aerosol
outer covering
penetration
without moisture
cannot
only hint
cannot fully

[the surviving alien walks at night]

each light world home
cannot trace
cannot backward recognize
come from cannot to
cannot go all here
which light
all here unrecognized

[the surviving alien contracts a fatal infection]

cannot track interior
cannot track increase
escalation
amplification
subliminal
as if through
as if filling

swarming
cannot work with

no mutuality
direction
concurrence
no penetration
synchronicity

cross-purposed

movement terminates
nutrition terminates
ingestion terminates

no entity in which to be absorbed

[alternative theory of the nature of aliens 1]

not body but mask
not mask but membrane
not membrane but seamless
deceiving touch
instruments
mind
hand plunged as if there

[alternative theory of the nature of aliens 2]

dream other universe
piercing through
not supposed accident
not supposed touch
dream how else
absorb prepare
dream solid
object dream

[alternative theory of the nature of aliens 3]

another form energy touch coalesce shock coalesce together planet coalesce assume parallel form not form coalesce severed counterfeit appearance coalesce severed cannot severed coalesce cannot

[alternative theory of the nature of aliens 4]

projection control
while elsewhere floating
or hands
control bar vertical
horizontal paddle control
pivots to allow
elsewhere select
opposite pull
bar and nuance attach

[alternative theory of the nature of aliens 5]

information sent lasers
interpret across need
device two devices
send receive what sent
collapses what received
revives

[alternative theory of the nature of aliens 6]

travelling in channel
manifest waveform
boundary angle
obstruction
complete

Afterword and sources:

These poems focus on the event/series of events in New Mexico in June/July 1947 in which debris, possibly from spaceships, possibly from Project Mogul balloons (designed to detect nuclear explosions), was found by Mac Brazel on the Foster Ranch near Corona in Chaves County, possibly by Lincoln LaPaz on another nearby ranch, and by a party including Gerald Anderson in a ravine on the Plains of San Augustin. A sighting near Mt. Rainier which anticipates the New Mexico events and supports both hypotheses is also included. The poems in the section Humans are redacted from testimonies and public documents listed below and make use of randomizing processes. The surviving alien poems attempt to be consistent with this testimony. I am grateful to Renee Carkin for introducing me to this material, and to Gerald Anderson for his kindness and patience in allowing me to interview him at length. Thanks also go to Francisco Irby, Cyrus Console, and my son, Ben Lombardo, for pointing me towards background information, and to Joe Harrington and Denise Low-Weso for many useful suggestions. And thanks always to my husband, Stanley Lombardo, for his support and meticulous editorial judgment.

The website http://www.thinkaboutitdocs.com/roswell-witness-testimonies/ was the source for testimony from the following:

Lydia A. Sleppy
the Brazel children
Walt Whitmore and the Marcels
Loretta Proctor
Robert Smith
Walter Haut
Robert Porter
the photographer F.B.
Bill Rickett
Barbara Dugger
Marian Strickland
Glenn Dennis

Ruben Anaya's testimony was taken from T*homas J. Carey and Donald R. Schmitt, Witness to Roswell*, New Page Books, Pompton Plains NJ, 2009.

Gerald Anderson's testimony is from a personal interview in May 2015.

Newspaper stories are either from *Witness to Roswell* or the *Air Force Roswell Report.*

Images of the FBI teletype can be found in many places online, among them http://www.project1947.com/roswell/fbi_tele.gif.

Kenneth Arnold's testimony can be found at http://www.project1947.com/fig/ka.htm.

The 994 page Air Force Roswell Report, which can be found at http://www.afhso.af.mil/shared/media/document/AFD-101201-038.pdf, was the source for the following:

Richard Neal's FOIA request
Irving Newton's testimony
the combined history of the 509th Bomb Group and the Roswell Army Air Field
Sheridan Cavitt's testimony
Marcia van Note's memorandum
Robert McCormick's memorandum
James Cole's memorandum
records searched during the Air Force investigation
the centers where records were searched
Maurice Ewing's memo
James Peoples' and Norman Haskell's memo
W.H. Congdon's memo
testimony from Athelstan Spilhaus
testimony from Charles Moore
testimony from Albert Trakowski
the summary of HQ NAIC research

The description of Project Mogul is from Wikipedia, and the basic science behind sound channels is from http://www.dosits.org/science/soundmovement/sofar/sofartravel/.

Finally, testimony that the surviving alien lived for 18 months in Los Alamos where it seemed drawn to walking at night, to walking in the pines, and to placing its hands in streams, came from Gerald Anderson, who heard it from Phillip Corso, who claimed to be the surviving alien's companion during those 18 months.

Judith Roitman has most recently published in *December*, *Rogue Agent*, *Galataea Resurrects*, *E.Ratio*, *The Writing Disorder*, *Otoliths*, *Eleven Eleven*, *Horse Less Review*, *Talisman*, and *Yew*. Her chapbooks include *Slackline* (Hank's Loose Gravel Press), *Furnace Mountain* (Omerta), *Ku: a thumb book* (Airfoil Press), and *Two: ghazals* (Horse Less Press). Her book *No Face: Selected and New Poems* (First Intensity) appeared in 2008. She lives in Lawrence, Kansas.

www.ingramcontent.com/pod-product-compliance
Lightning Source LLC
Chambersburg PA
CBHW020702300426
44112CB00007B/481
* 9 7 8 0 9 8 8 3 8 9 1 5 1 *